KU-220-359

Contents

WANDSWORTH LIBRARY SERVICE

The river bank

A grassy bank slopes down to the river. Sunlight sparkles on the water.

By the edge

A wooden fence protects
the edge of the muddy bank.

A duck stands on a fallen branch and keeps an eye on its ducklings.

Fishing

Two boys are fishing with rods and lines.

They use maggots for bait. They put the fish they catch back in the water.

A bend in the river

The stone bridge is a road bridge for cars and other traffic.

Tall reeds grow by the bank
where the river bends.

Wide and slow

After the bend, the river becomes wider. The water flows slowly.

Water lilies grow in the slow part of the river.

The river divides

Gardens run right down
to the river bank.

The river divides and becomes two rivers.

The weir

A weir crosses the river
from bank to bank.

Water rushes over
the weir.
Below the weir,
the river is fast
and shallow.

Bridges

From the footbridge you can see reflections in the water.

A train crosses the strong metal railway bridge.

How are the bridges across the river different?

The big river

Boats can slide down the concrete ramp into the water.

The little river has joined the big river and flows towards the city.
What is the heron looking for?

Houseboats

People live on houseboats that are moored on the big river.

There is a paved path and a metal fence along the bank.

How else have the river and the bank changed from the start of the walk?

Map

You can start a walk from any point on a map. To follow the walk in this book, put your finger on **Start** and trace the route.

Key

ducks

fishermen

reeds

water lilies

houses

weir

bridge

ramp

houseboats

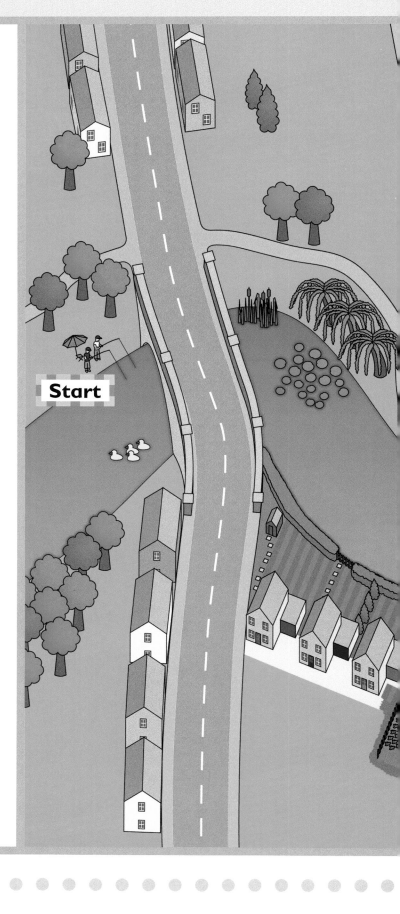

Start

Quiz

Ducklings swim on the river. What other animals live in the water?

Look at pages 10 and 11.

A road bridge crosses the river. What other bridges cross the river?

Look at pages 18, 20, 21 and 25.

A weir is like a dam across the river.
How does it change the way the river flows?

Look at pages 18 and 19.

A wooden fence runs along
the bank.
What else can you find
in the water by the bank?

Look at pages 9, 13 and 15.

People enjoy a ride along
the river.
What have they
sailed past?

Look at page 23.

Houseboats float close together.
How do people get to their
houseboats?

Look at page 24.

Index

501342017

Always go for a walk with an adult. Take care around water.

First published in 2005 by
Franklin Watts
96 Leonard Street
London, EC2A 4XD

Franklin Watts Australia
45-51 Huntley Street
Alexandria, NSW 2015

© Franklin Watts 2005

Editors: Caryn Jenner, Sarah Ridley
Designer: Louise Best
Art director: Jonathan Hair
Photography: Chris Fairclough
Map: Hardlines

Many thanks to Heather, Roger, Emily and Harriet Cox for agreeing to appear in the book.

A CIP catalogue record for this book is available from the British Library

ISBN 0 7496 6040 6

All rights reserved. No part of this publication may be reproduced, stored in a retrieval system, or transmitted in any form or by any means, electronic, mechanical, photocopy, recording or otherwise, without the prior written permission of the copyright owner.

Printed in China

A walk by the River

Written by Sally Hewitt
Photography by Chris Fairclough

W

FRANKLIN WATTS
LONDON • SYDNEY

501 342 017